At a Glance™ Series

DVD and Lesson Book

DVD Scales and Modes

Written by Mike Mueller, Barrett Tagliarino & Chad Johnson
Video Performers: Doug Boduch & Troy Stetina

ISBN 978-1-4234-3308-8

HAL•LEONARD®
CORPORATION
7777 W. BLUEMOUND RD. P.O. BOX 13819 MILWAUKEE, WI 53213

Visit Hal Leonard Online at
www.halleonard.com

Table of Contents

INTRODUCTION

Welcome to *Guitar Scales and Modes*, from Hal Leonard's exciting new At a Glance series. Not as "scholarly" or formal as traditional method books, the material in *Guitar Scales and Modes* is presented in a snappy and fun manner intended to have you playing scales of all types in virtually no time at all. Plus, the At a Glance series uses real songs by real artists to illustrate how the concepts you're learning are applied in some of the biggest hits of all time. For example, in *Guitar Scales and Modes*, you'll learn riffs and licks from over 20 rock, pop, and blues classics, including Jimi Hendrix's "Hey Joe," ZZ Top's "La Grange," Led Zeppelin's "Babe, I'm Gonna Leave You," and Eric Johnson's "Cliffs of Dover."

Additionally, each book in the At a Glance series comes with a DVD containing video lessons that correspond to the printed material. The DVD that accompanies this book contains four video lessons, each approximately 8 to 10 minutes in length, that correspond to each chapter in *Guitar Scales and Modes*. In these videos, ace instructors will show you in great detail everything from variations on major scale fingerings to the difference between the Lydian and Ionian modes. As you go through *Guitar Scales and Modes*, try to play the examples first on your own, and then check out the DVD for additional help or to see if you played it correctly. As the saying goes, "A picture is worth a thousand words," so be sure to use this invaluable tool on your quest to becoming the consummate lead guitarist.

THE MAJOR SCALE

The major scale is the foundation for all styles of Western music, from classical and jazz to the most extreme metal. We use it to construct chords, define keys, and build melodies and solos—it's essentially the frame of reference we use to describe all note relationships. Which makes it pretty obvious how important it is for every musician to know it, and know it well.

Though it can sound completely different depending on the musical style, or the way it is used in a particular song, the major scale always follows a strict pattern of notes called the *major scale formula*. Comprising seven notes in a series of whole- (W) and half-step (H) intervals, the formula looks like this:

```
1 – 2 – 3 – 4 – 5 – 6 – 7 – 1
 \ / \ / \ / \ / \ / \ / \ /
 W   W   H   W   W   W   H
```

As you can see, the notes of the major scale are numbered 1–7. Each number represents a scale *degree*. You'll hear these scale degrees commonly referred to as, for example, the "3rd," or the "5th." Additionally, the first note of a major scale is called the *tonic* (or *root*). This is the "home" tone on which most melodies end.

An easy way to see and learn this formula on the guitar is to first play it on just one string. We'll use a C major scale, to start, as it contains no sharp or flat notes (more on that shortly). In the key of C, the tonic is C. So place your fret hand's index finger on the fifth string, at the third fret, to play the tonic, and then slide your finger up the fifth string according to the major scale formula of whole and half steps, until you reach the *octave* C note at the fifteenth fret (numbered as "8"). Move your finger up two frets for a whole step, and one fret for a half step.

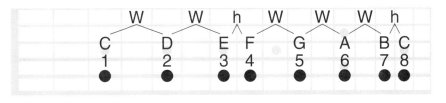

NATURAL HALF STEPS, SHARPS, AND FLATS

In the C major scale you just played, the interval between the notes E and F, and B and C, is a naturally occurring half step, which means they're half-step intervals that occur without the use of sharp or flat notes (more on that in a minute). This is important to remember as you now begin to build other major scales, because starting on any note other than C requires the use of sharps and flats.

When a note is made *sharp*, this symbol [♯] appears next to it, and it sounds one half step higher in pitch. On a guitar, you simply play it one fret higher. When a note is made *flat*, this symbol [♭] appears next to the note name, and it sounds one half step lower. On the guitar, you slide your finger back one fret.

Notice that both F♯ and G♭ are played on the sixth string at the second fret. When two notes have different names but sound the same pitch, they are called *enharmonic equivalents*. The reason these exist is that when you spell a major scale in a sharp key, all the notes must be named as sharps, and in a flat key, they must be named as flats. But you shouldn't concern yourself with those details this early in the game. Just know that it's OK for two notes to sound the same.

As the word "formula" implies, the major scale blueprint of whole steps and half steps can be applied to any note to create that tonic's major scale. So let's apply the major scale formula to the tonic F, to create an F major scale. To begin, place your index finger on the sixth string at the first fret and then follow the formula.

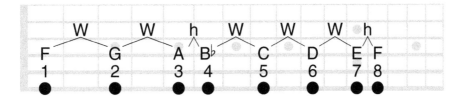

As you can see, the F major scale contains one flatted note, B♭. That pitch can also be called A♯, but one of the rules you must follow when building a major scale is that you use each letter name only once. Using this rule plus the major scale formula will allow you to spell the major scale starting from any tonic note.

Let's do one more, this time, starting with the open D string.

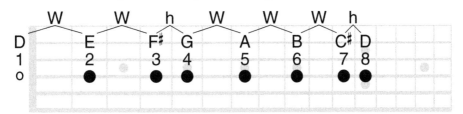

Open-Position C Major Scale

So far, we've played the major scale only in a linear pattern, or along just one string. But if you've ever watched the guitarist in a music video, you've probably noticed that they don't often play up and down the neck on just one string! In fact, scales are most often played across multiple strings instead of on just one. It's a little harder to see the whole and half steps this way, but it's obviously easier to play.

To demonstrate, we'll begin with a C major scale in *open position*, which means you'll be using open strings. Here first is a diagram of what the pattern looks like on the fretboard, with the C notes circled. Then you'll see the pattern laid out in tablature, to play along with the demonstration on the accompanying DVD.

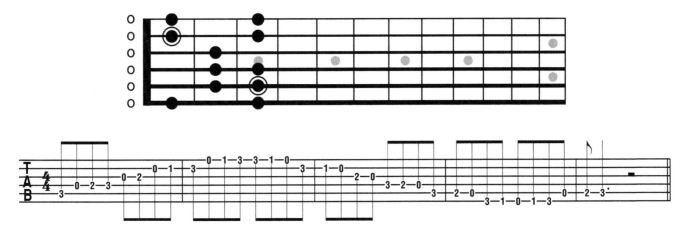

Practice the pattern up and down, starting and stopping only on the root, for a few minutes a day, until it is so familiar to your fingers that you can play it starting from any note and continue up or down the pattern at will.

Let's try a familiar melody from "The First Noël" using the open-position C major scale. While this song is pretty easy to play—moving up and down the scale with almost no skipping around—it does include some rhythmic variations you may not have learned about yet. Don't worry about sight-reading the rhythms for now—you'll likely remember this melody anyway. If you don't know it, listen and play along with the DVD.

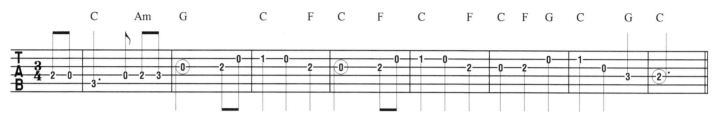

Movable Major Scale Fingerings

You're obviously not going to spend your entire guitar-playing career in open position, so you'll need to learn some movable major scale fingerings, too. As you may have guessed, movable major scale patterns contain no open strings, which in turn pumps up the workload on your fretting hand.

In this lesson, we're going to explore five movable shapes, based on the open-position shapes of the C, A, G, E, and D major chords. This is called the *CAGED* system. The first movable major scale fingering we're going to explore is based on the open A major chord shape. For the most part, we'll use *box patterns*, which means you assign one fret-hand finger to each fret in a four-fret area.

A-Form Pattern

Since you're quickly becoming familiar with the C major scale, let's stick with it. To begin, let's use the same C root, on the fifth string at the third fret, only this time, fret the note with your second finger, and then follow the "A-form" pattern below. It's named the A-form because the C major barre chord present in this shape on strings 5–2 resembles the open A major chord. Note that this isn't a strict box pattern, in that you need to shift your hand position up one fret when you reach the second string. Watch the instructor on the accompanying DVD to see how to smoothly execute this move. Once you're comfortable with the pattern, try adding the notes in parentheses on the sixth and first strings, using your index and pinky fingers, respectively, to fret them.

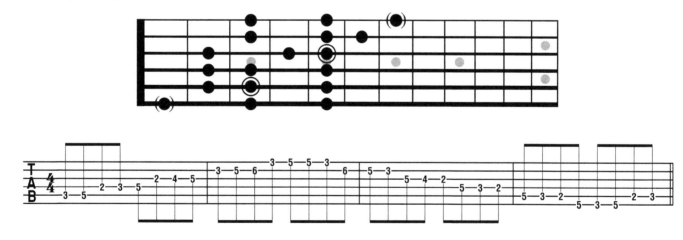

You can move this pattern up and down the fretboard to any root note and play its associated major scale. For example, shift the pattern up two frets, and you're playing a D major scale.

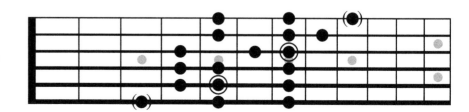

G-Form Pattern

The next movable major scale pattern is based on the open G chord shape. In this pattern, the root—C, as shown here—is on the sixth string, fretted with your pinky finger. Additionally, there are two ways to play this scale. Before you begin playing it, look at the diagram and find the B notes in parentheses on the fourth and third strings. As you play this scale, you will choose only *one* of those notes. You can either stretch your pinky finger out to reach the B on the fourth string at the ninth fret, OR, you can shift your hand position back one fret for the three notes on the third string, and then back up one fret when you reach the second string. To best aid you in future guitar endeavors, you should get *both* patterns confidently under your fingers.

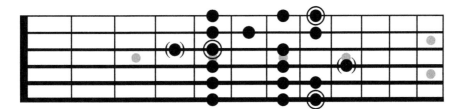

ALTERNATE PICKING

Though it's a matter of debate in some circles, it's generally agreed upon that *alternate picking* is the most efficient way to navigate single-note lines and scale patterns. Using this method, you alternate downstrokes [⊓] and upstrokes [∨] to get through the scale or phrase at hand. For example, here's the A major scale in a G-form pattern, with picking directions beneath the tab.

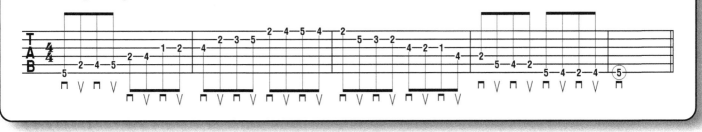

As we mentioned in the beginning of this lesson, knowing and understanding the major scale is essential to building chords, and practicing major scales is a wonderful way to reinforce that knowledge while developing pick- and fret-hand coordination. But the main reason people want to learn how to play scales is so they can begin playing *solos!* Let's face it: rhythm guitarists may do 90 percent of the work, but *lead* guitarists get 90 percent of the spotlight, so let's learn a couple of licks.

A *lick* is a short, melodic statement, typically composed of single notes. This first one uses a popular phrasing tool called a *sequence* to descend the G form of the C major scale in four-note groupings. You'll hear this one most often in hard rock solos.

And next up is the harmony part to one of the most famous major scale licks of all time: the Allman Brothers Band's "Jessica." This second guitar part is based in the G-form of the A major scale. By the way, we'll take a look at the primary guitar lick shortly, when we learn the D-form pattern of the major scale.

"JESSICA"
Allman Brothers Band

Written by Dickey Betts

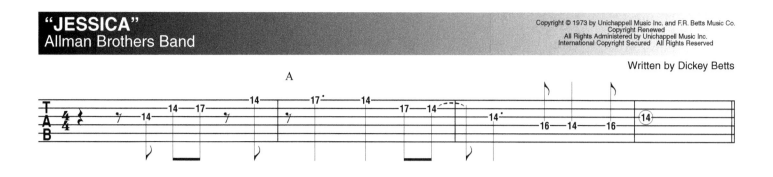

E-Form Pattern

Based on the shape of the open E major chord, this next major scale pattern is usually the first one that guitarists learn. This pattern's root is found on the sixth string, under your fret hand's middle finger. Staying in the key of C major, that means the root is on the sixth string, at the eighth fret. This pattern is a strict *box* pattern, with no finger stretches or hand shifts required.

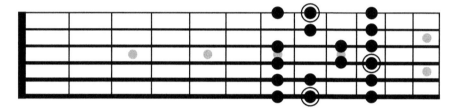

Here's a scale exercise using the E-form pattern. Moving up the neck chromatically, this exercise is a wonderful alternate picking workout. Be sure to use a metronome and use a tempo at which you can play the exercise perfectly. Once you've climbed up the neck to the fifteenth fret (one octave), kick up the tempo a notch or two and reverse direction.

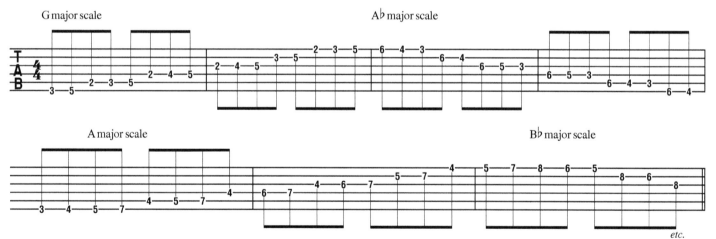

Guitarist Neil Geraldo uses the top two strings of this pattern to open his E-major solo in Pat Benatar's "Hit Me with Your Best Shot."

"HIT ME WITH YOUR BEST SHOT"
Pat Benatar

Words and Music by
Eddie Schwartz

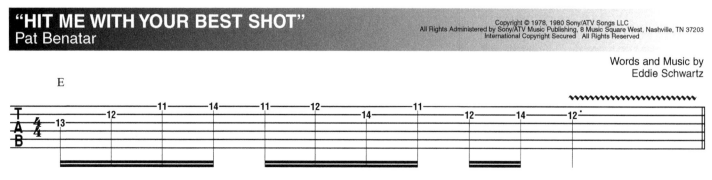

D-Form Pattern

The next major scale pattern comes from the open D major chord shape. In this pattern, the root is on the fourth string, played with your index finger. This shape is also known as the Dorian mode scale pattern (see Modes, page 26), but that version starts on a different root. Stretch your fret hand's pinky finger to reach the notes at the fourteenth fret on the fifth and fourth strings. Alternatively, you can ignore those two notes and instead play them on the fourth and third strings, respectively, at the ninth fret. This approach will require a position shift, but it's worth learning both shapes.

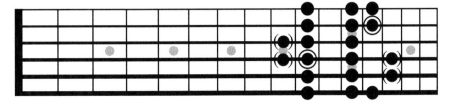

Now, as promised, here's the primary guitar melody from the Allman Brothers Band's "Jessica," which comes from the D-form pattern.

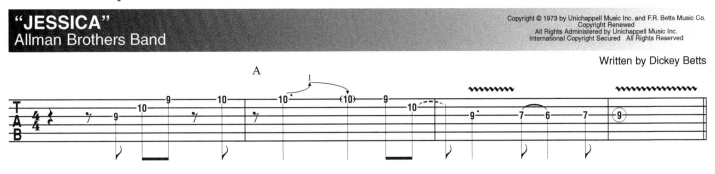

"JESSICA"
Allman Brothers Band

Written by Dickey Betts

C-Form Pattern

You may not realize it, but you already learned the C-form pattern when you learned the open-position C major scale. All you need to do is move that scale up one fret and substitute notes on the first fret for the open strings, and you've got the movable pattern. Here, it's presented again in the key of C major, one octave higher.

The C-form major scale pattern is one of the most popular shapes in rock guitar; however, it's typically employed as a minor scale, using the same finger pattern but a different root—more on that in the next chapter. Meanwhile, here's one of the most famous major scale licks using this pattern.

"BOHEMIAN RHAPSODY"
Queen

Words and Music by
Freddie Mercury

Now let's take a look at some other rock and pop hits that use these various major scale patterns.

Eric Johnson caps off his famous unaccompanied intro to "Cliffs of Dover" with a blazing G major scale run, finishing off with an incredible five-note pattern from G major pentatonic.

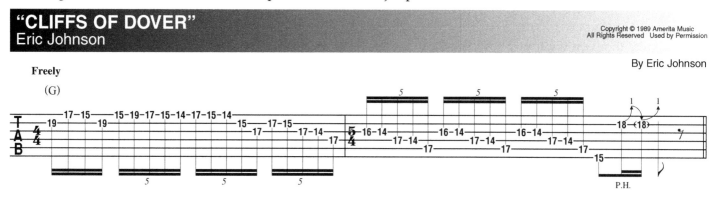

Another classic lick using the D-form pattern is heard in the Beatles' timeless ballad "And I Love Her."

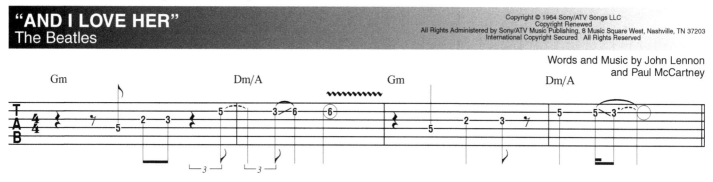

Boston's Tom Sholz is practically the king of major scale soloing. Here's the opening to his classic solo from "More than a Feeling," which makes melodic use of the D major scale.

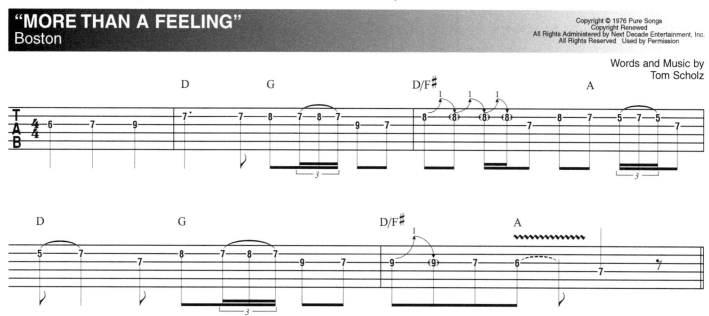

THE MINOR SCALE

Technically speaking, any scale with a flatted 3rd degree is a minor scale, but in this lesson, we're going to focus on the natural minor scale. To fully understand the natural minor scale, it is helpful to first compare it to the major scale. As you learned in the last chapter, the major scale contains seven notes, or scale degrees, arranged in a pattern of whole and half steps, numbered generically 1 through 7.

$$1 - 2 - 3 - 4 - 5 - 6 - 7 - 1$$
$$\setminus \ / \setminus \ / \setminus \ / \setminus \ / \setminus \ / \setminus \ / \setminus \ /$$
$$\text{W} \quad \text{W} \quad \text{H} \quad \text{W} \quad \text{W} \quad \text{W} \quad \text{H}$$

Now, to convert that to a minor scale pattern, we apply the minor scale formula, which calls for flatted 3rd, 6th, and 7th scale degrees.

$$1 - 2 - \flat3 - 4 - 5 - \flat6 - \flat7 - 1$$
$$\setminus \ / \setminus \ / \setminus \ / \setminus \ / \setminus \ / \setminus \ / \setminus \ /$$
$$\text{W} \quad \text{H} \quad \text{W} \quad \text{W} \quad \text{H} \quad \text{W} \quad \text{W}$$

If, for example, you apply this to the A major scale (A–B–C♯–D–E–F♯–G♯), the 3rd, C♯, becomes a ♭3rd, C; the 6th, F♯, is flatted to F; and the 7th, G♯, goes down to G. So the A minor scale is spelled A–B–C–D–E–F–G.

Using the E-form major scale pattern, let's apply this formula to the fretboard. Begin with the major scale pattern…

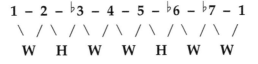

but play the 3rd, 6th, and 7th notes of the scale one fret behind, so that the pattern now looks like this:

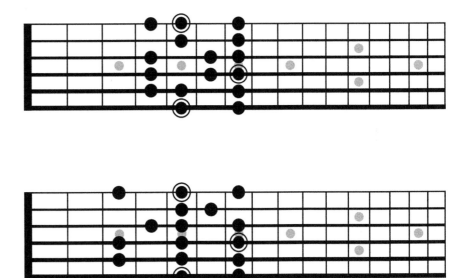

There are some pretty big finger stretches in that pattern, but it illustrates the difference between the major and minor patterns. Here is a much simpler and more common finger pattern for the minor scale. This one, based on the open Em chord shape, contains the same notes as the previous one, just in more convenient fretboard locations.

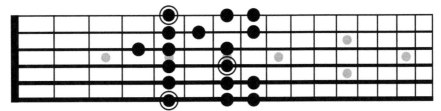

This pattern, like its major scale cousin, is a *movable* pattern with the root note played by your index finger on the low E string, which means all you need to do to play a different minor scale is shift your index finger to that scale's root. For example, if you want to play a B minor scale, just slide your index finger from the fifth fret up to the seventh fret, and then play the pattern.

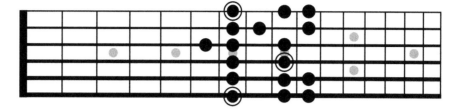

To get this minor scale pattern under your fingers, practice playing it up and down the fretboard in ascending and descending directions. To get you started, follow the pattern shown here. Be sure to use alternate picking in this and all of the scale exercises to come.

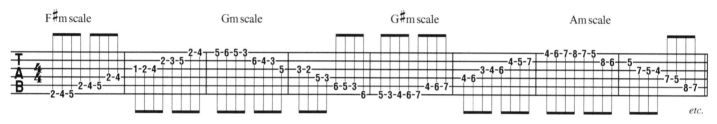

Relative Minor Scale

When you flatted the 3rd, 6th, and 7th degrees of the major scale to form a minor scale, you created a *parallel* minor scale; that is, a minor scale with the same root as the major scale from which it was derived.

Another type of minor scale is the *relative* minor. The relative minor scale contains the *same notes* as its relative major scale—there are no flatted degrees—but you start on the 6th scale degree. I know, it sounds confusing, but once you get the hang of it, you'll find the relative minor approach invaluable when improvising.

To better understand the concept, let's look at an example using the A major scale we used at the beginning of this chapter to create its parallel A minor scale. Recall that the A major scale is spelled: A–B–C♯–D–E–F♯–G♯, with those notes numbered 1–7, respectively. Now, if you count up to the 6th scale degree, which is F♯, and then play the notes of the A major scale from F♯ to F♯, you're playing A major's relative minor scale—F♯ minor (F♯–G♯–A–B–C♯–D–E).

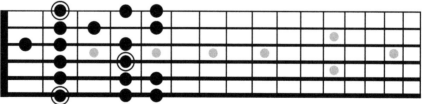

The relative minor is very useful to rock guitarists, as traditionally, most popular rock guitar phrases are based on minor scale fingerings. And if you're playing over a major chord progression and want to use some of those licks, you'll need to be able to find the relative minor scale pattern.

Rather than counting up to the 6th and then reordering scale tones, an easier way to find the relative minor scale in a major key is to locate the major scale root on the fretboard, then move back *three* frets, and the resulting note is the relative minor scale root. Once you're there, simply play the minor scale finger pattern.

Minor Scale Licks

OK, it's time to take a look at some minor scale licks. All of these licks are presented here in A minor. But just like the scale pattern, these licks are also movable, meaning you can slide them up or down the fretboard as necessary to accommodate the key you're in.

 This first lick is a popular rock guitar motif that uses pull-offs to great effect. Be careful not to rush the pull-offs.

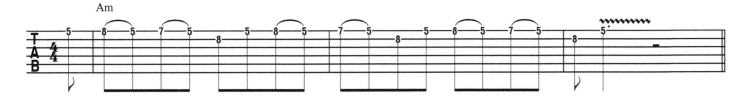

 The second lick uses a descending sequence of four-note groupings before landing on the root, A.

 The next lick begins with a whole-step bend up to the root, A, and then sequences down the A minor scale in triplets.

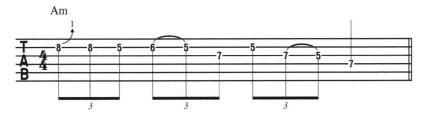

The next lick kicks off with a pre-bend. If you have trouble hitting the target note, C, on the pre-bend, first play the fretted C note at the eighth fret, and then bend the seventh-fret B up to C, repeatedly, until your fingers know just how far to push up the string to hit the correct pitch.

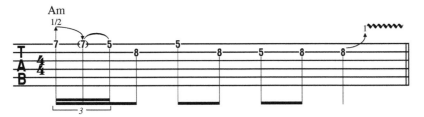

Try playing each of these licks in other popular rock keys, such as B minor, C# minor, and E minor, to help you get these licks under your fingers.

Next, for an example of real-world application, here's the Em-form scale shape as heard in some killer hard rock classics.

Yngwie Malmsteen made use of the E minor scale in this blazing arpeggio pull-off lick from "Rising Force." With a tempo of 248 b.p.m., absolute economy of motion is necessary to execute the sixteenth notes.

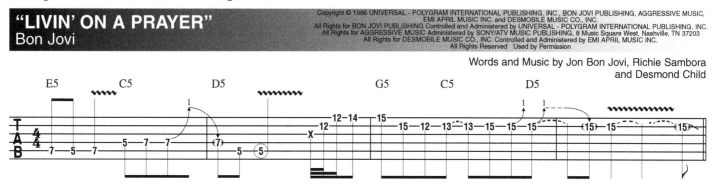

"I'LL SEE THE LIGHT TONIGHT"
Yngwie Malmsteen

Words and Music by Yngwie Malmsteen
and Jeff Scott Soto

In 1986, New Jersey rockers Bon Jovi climbed to the top of the hair metal heap on the strength of its monster album, *Slippery When Wet*. One of the singles responsible for the band's commercial breakthrough was "Livin' on a Prayer," which featured guitarist Richie Sambora resurrecting the talk-box effect and using the Em-form scale pattern to create the following memorable motif.

"LIVIN' ON A PRAYER"
Bon Jovi

Words and Music by Jon Bon Jovi, Richie Sambora
and Desmond Child

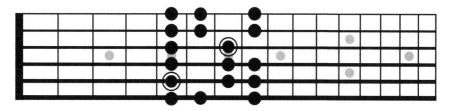

Am-Form Movable Minor Scale Shape

The Em-form minor scale pattern, with its root on the 6th string, is one of the two most commonly used minor scale shapes. The other is the Am-form shape, which is the same as the C-form major scale pattern, with its root on the fifth string, but under your *index* finger. Here's what that one looks like, shown here at the fifth fret, which makes it a D minor scale.

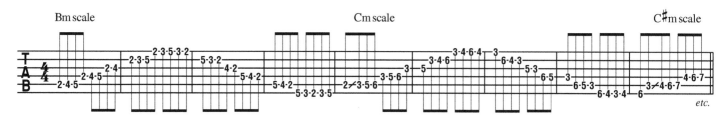

Like the Em-form pattern, the Am-form minor scale shape is a movable one. Here's a chromatically ascending exercise similar to the one you used on the Em-form pattern, to help you get comfortable with this scale pattern. As always, use alternate picking and a metronome. When you get up to the fourteenth fret, play the pattern and then reverse direction and descend the neck back to second position.

More Licks!

Now let's learn some licks from the Am-form scale pattern.

While the first lick looks like nothing more than a walk up the A minor scale in twelfth position, it's essentially the move that Metallica guitarist Kirk Hammett used to close out his intro solo to their breakthrough metal hit "Fade to Black."

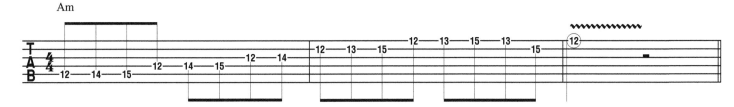

This next lick uses a descending sequence of triplets in the A minor scale. This is actually another of Kirk Hammett's favorite moves.

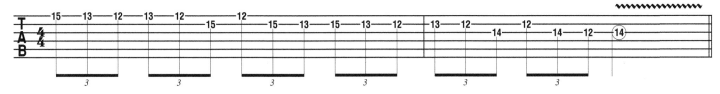

For the next lick, we'll move down the fretboard to seventh position and the key of E minor. This one is very similar to the first lick from the Em-form section of this lesson, so it should feel pretty comfortable.

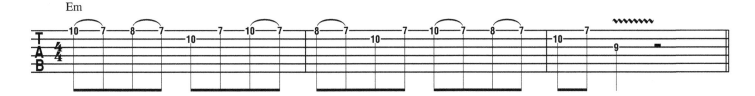

For the next minor scale lick, we're going to take it up a notch. This lick, variations of which have been used by such diverse guitarists as Kirk Hammett, Carlos Santana, and Brian Setzer, uses a repeating sextuplet motif combined with pull-offs.

A *sextuplet* is a rhythmic value that squeezes six notes into the space of a single beat. It may look a little intimidating at first, but I think you'll be surprised at how simple it really is. If you're having trouble with the rhythm, you can think of each sextuplet as two sixteenth-note triplets per beat.

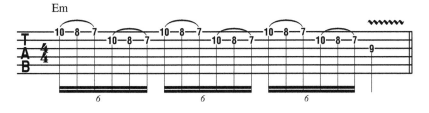

Now, to close out this lesson on the minor scale, let's take a look at some famous riffs and licks that use the fifth-string-rooted Am-form scale.

The first example is the opening phrase from Jimmy Page's nylon-string solo in Led Zeppelin's "Babe, I'm Gonna Leave You."

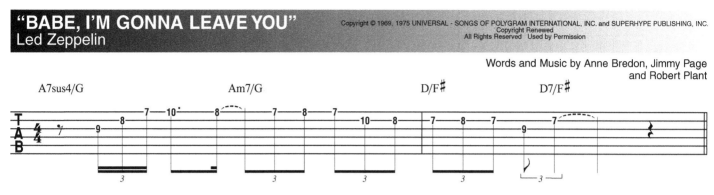

A few years earlier, British psychedelic prog-rockers Pink Floyd released *Dark Side of the Moon*, which turned the music world on its ear with its eerie, atmospheric sounds and amazing arrangements. One of the album's hits, "Money," is anchored by a 7/4 riff in B minor, played in second position.

In 1976, a little band out of Boston, called Boston, released their debut album titled, er, *Boston*, which would go on to become one of the best-selling rock 'n' roll records of all time. And the intro theme to one of its biggest hits, "Peace of Mind," just happened to use our new scale pattern, in the key of C♯ minor.

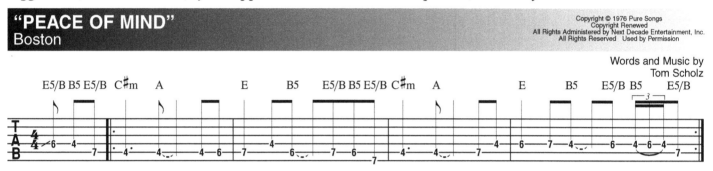

A few years earlier, British psychedelic prog-rockers Pink Floyd released *Dark Side of the Moon*, which turned the music world on its ear with its eerie, atmospheric sounds and amazing arrangements. One of the album's hits, "Money," is anchored by a 7/4 riff in B minor, played in second position.

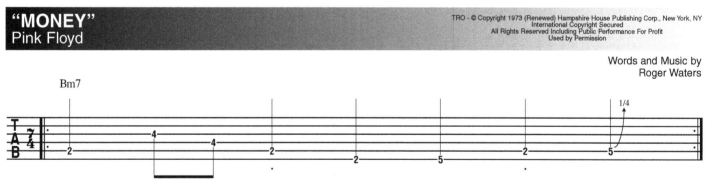

For our last minor key riff, we go back all the way to 1960 and the age of surf music, for the Ventures' timeless "Walk Don't Run," an instrumental whose main riff is a simple walk up the A minor scale. Although it's played in open position, the scale shape is the same as the fretted one you've been using, with open strings substituting for notes fretted with your index finger.

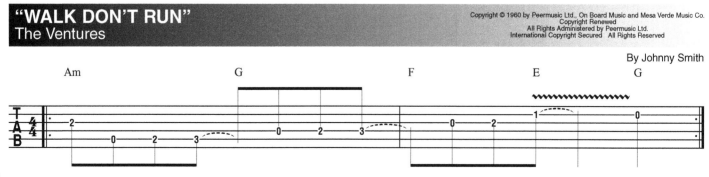

THE MINOR PENTATONIC SCALE

If guitarists the world over had to pick the one scale they use most often and with which they feel most comfortable, you can rest assured it would be the *minor pentatonic*. Through the years, this ubiquitous collection of notes has formed the foundation of some of the greatest solos and riffs in blues, country, rock, and pop music, and it's still going strong today.

The word "pentatonic" derives from the Greek word *penta*, meaning "five," and *tonic*, meaning "note," which simply means the minor pentatonic scale contains five notes. Again using the major scale as the foundation, the five notes of the minor pentatonic scale are the root, flatted 3rd, 4th, 5th, and flatted 7th (1–$\flat3$–4–5–$\flat7$). You can also think of it as the natural minor scale minus the 2nd and 6th scale degrees.

Using the latter method, let's build an A minor pentatonic scale from the A natural minor scale. Recall that the A minor scale is spelled:

A–B–C–D–E–F–G

Now, if you remove the 2nd, B, and the 6th, F, you're left with these five notes:

A–C–D–E–G

The resulting sound is one that is not quite as "dark" as the minor scale, with the added benefit of making it easier *not* to hit a "bad note" while improvising.

The Minor Pentatonic Box

Just as there are five notes in the minor pentatonic scale, there are five scale shapes associated with it. But one of those shapes has been used far more than any other, and it's the root-position minor pentatonic box, shown here in fifth position, making it an A minor pentatonic scale.

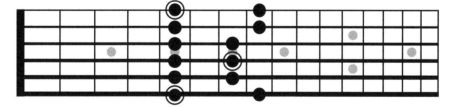

This two-octave shape has been the basis for countless licks throughout the years—like these:

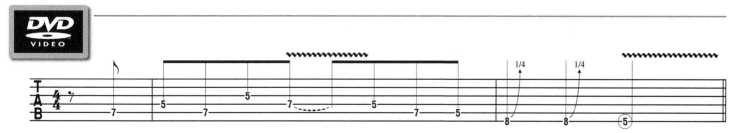

As you play through the licks and exercises in this chapter, stick to a box-pattern fingering, where you play all the notes on the fifth fret with your fret hand's index finger, of course, and all the seventh-fret notes with your ring finger, and all the eighth-fret notes with your pinky finger.

That being said, many guitarists prefer to use their ring finger to play the notes at the eighth fret on the top two strings. We suggest you practice playing the scale *both* ways, as each has its advantages (and disadvantages).

Now, before we get into playing licks, let's go through some exercises to help get the minor pentatonic box under your fingers. This first one is a triplet sequence that descends through the scale form. Use alternate picking throughout the exercise, and for now, stick to a strict box pattern fingering, using your pinky finger on the first, second, and sixth strings.

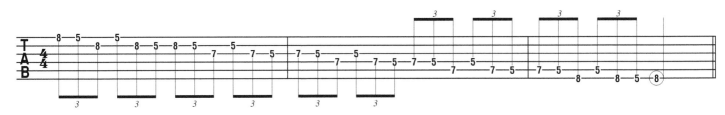

And now, moving in the opposite direction, this next exercise takes the minor pentatonic scale through an ascending sequence of triplets.

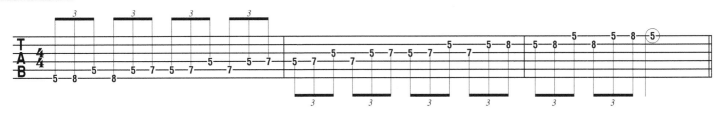

Our third exercise ascends through the minor pentatonic box shape four strings at a time. Be careful with your picking on this one; you'll be skipping a string at the beginning of each new measure.

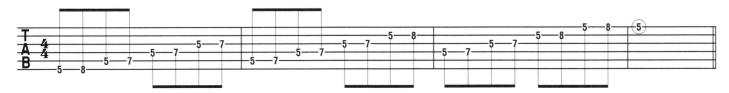

Now let's reverse directions and descend the scale pattern four strings at a time, again skipping a string with each new measure.

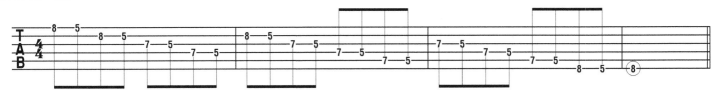

Minor Pentatonic Licks

Now the fun begins. Every guitarist should have an arsenal of "stock" licks from which to choose when in an improvisation setting. In this next section, we're going to help you start building that arsenal with some essential minor pentatonic moves.

Since you've been playing all of your minor pentatonic exercises in fifth position, we'll stick to licks in the key of A minor for now. As always, use alternate picking to navigate these licks. Here's the first one:

 The next lick introduces *double stops*, or two notes played at the same time. Alternate picking is still the name of the game, but you'll need to pay special attention to the transition between single notes and double stops.

One way to add a little pizzazz to a lick is to *slide* into a note. In this next example, there are two slides present. In the first bar, you'll slide up to the seventh fret, on the fourth string. And in the second bar, you'll slide down to the fifth fret, on the fifth string.

 There is no predetermined starting point for these slides, but a general rule of thumb is to begin the slide one or two frets away from the target note. Be sure to execute the slide rather quickly, so as not to give the notes you're sliding through any rhythmic space.

The next lick introduces a new sliding technique called a *shift slide*, where two or more notes are connected by a straight line indicating the direction of the slide along with a curved line called a *slur*, which indicates that only the first note is struck. In this particular lick, begin with your ring finger on the fifth string at the fifth fret, strike the note, and then slide up to the seventh fret but don't restrike the string when you get there.

This lick also introduces you to techniques called hammer-ons and pull-offs. To execute a *hammer-on*, strike the first note under the slur, and then "hammer" the appropriate fret-hand finger onto the target fret indicated at the end of the slur. To play a *pull-off*, strike the first note under the slur as usual, but make sure the target note is already fretted behind the struck note, and then "pull" your front finger off the string, with a gentle plucking action, to sound the lower-fretted note.

 If this all seems a little confusing, watch the instructor on the DVD closely. And don't worry, in the case of hammer-ons and pull-offs, it's easier *done* than said!

String Bending

We've begun to tackle such dynamic moves as slides, hammer-ons, and pull-offs, but probably the most common expressive technique used in conjunction with the minor pentatonic scale is *string bending*. In the minor pentatonic box pattern, there are two primary bends. The first is a whole-step bend from the 4th degree up to the 5th degree, which is done with your fret-hand's ring finger on the third string.

The other is a whole-step bend from the ♭7th up to the tonic, or root. In the box, this is performed with your fret hand's pinky finger on the second string. Be sure to use your fret hand's middle and ring fingers to reinforce your pinky in making the bend.

The most important element in string bending is making sure your bends are in tune. To help you consistently reach your target, first play the target pitch as a fretted note, keep that pitch in mind, and then execute the string bend up to that pitch. For a whole-step bend, the target pitch is the note two frets higher than the bent note. So in the previous example, you would first play the note at the tenth fret of the second string, then fret the eighth fret, strike the note and bend the string until its pitch matches that of the fretted tenth fret.

OK, let's try these string bends in some minor pentatonic licks! Used by everyone from Chuck Berry to Eric Clapton to Kirk Hammett, this first lick is an absolute must-have in your bag of tricks.

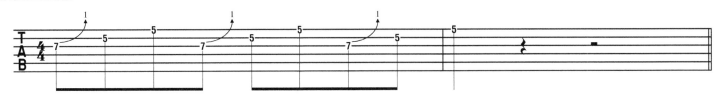

This next lick uses both of the bends shown above. Notice that for the bend in bar 2, you execute a *bend-and-release* move, in which you raise and lower the pitch by a whole step, in time.

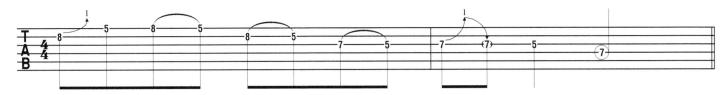

Playing in Other Keys

So far we've stuck with the A minor pentatonic scale, for demonstration purposes. But one of the many beauties of the minor pentatonic box shape is that it's movable. For example, if you move the box pattern up just two frets, so that the root note is under your index finger at the seventh fret, you get the B minor pentatonic scale.

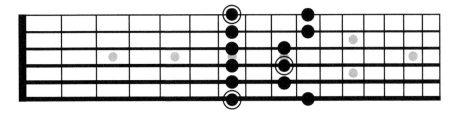

Just as the minor pentatonic box pattern is movable, so is every lick you've learned so far. Go back and try playing them in other popular rock keys, like B minor (seventh position), D minor (tenth position), and E minor (twelfth position). Meanwhile, here's a new must-know lick, this time using the B minor pentatonic scale, in seventh position.

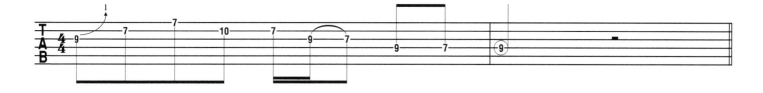

And here's one using the D minor pentatonic box pattern, in tenth position. Note that the opening bend tosses you a bit of a curveball. To play this one, play the fretted note at the twelfth fret, allowing it to ring for the duration of an eighth note, and then bend it up a whole step, reaching the target pitch on the "and" of beat 1.

Also, the final quarter note in measure 1 introduces a *quarter-step bend*. To play this kind of bend, you're not really bending to a target pitch so much as simply "nudging" the string slightly sharp, to give the note a more vocal flavor.

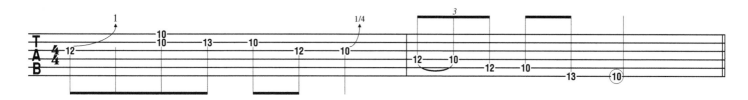

This next example moves the pattern up to twelfth position, making it an E minor pentatonic scale. It also offers two variations on one of the most popular stock licks ever played.

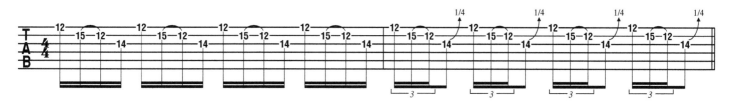

OK, now that you've been working on stock licks from the minor pentatonic box pattern, let's take a look at how some of the greatest guitarists of all time have put this handy pattern to work.

The first example comes from the one and only Jimi Hendrix. In his classic version of "Hey Joe," Hendrix kicks off his solo with a whole-step bend from the ♭7th, D, to the tonic, E, and then follows it up with that last stock lick you learned, before repeating the motif in the second bar.

"HEY JOE"
Jimi Hendrix

Words and Music by
Billy Roberts

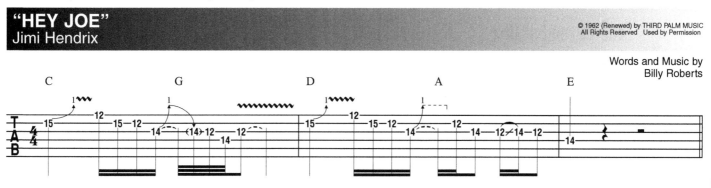

Eric "Slow Hand" Clapton has crafted a 40-plus year career largely on his ability to turn the minor pentatonic scale into pure rock magic. And while he's best known for his long and storied solo career as well as his legendary work in Cream, some of his most fiery guitar playing is heard on John Mayall's *Blues Breakers with Eric Clapton*, from 1966. Here is the main riff to "Steppin' Out," an instrumental blues-rocker in the key of G.

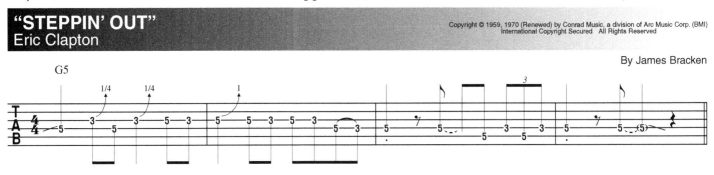

By James Bracken

Before that "li'l ol' band from Texas" became known for the hot chicks and even hotter 1932 Ford hot rod in their landmark 1980s MTV videos, ZZ Top was one of the grittiest, hard-rockin' blues bands on the circuit. Below, you'll find one of the most recognizable descending minor pentatonic licks of all time—the first few bars of Billy F. Gibbons' solo in "La Grange."

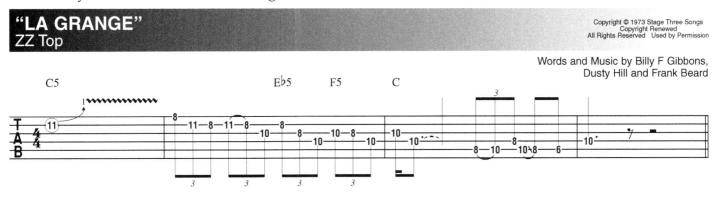

Words and Music by Billy F Gibbons,
Dusty Hill and Frank Beard

If there's anyone with a total command of the minor pentatonic scale, it's undoubtedly Eric Johnson, and he demonstrates nothing less with this blazing F minor pentatonic run from "Righteous," which he crams in between some chordal playing during the song's head without missing a beat.

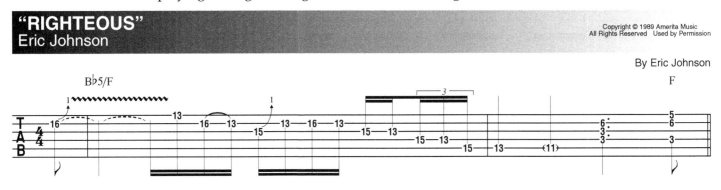

By Eric Johnson

The Extended Box

You should be feeling pretty comfortable with the minor pentatonic box pattern by now, so let's raise the bar a bit. As we mentioned at the start of this chapter, there are five minor pentatonic scale patterns. And although we're focusing only on the root-position box shape for this lesson, there is a common extension to that box position, borrowed from one of the other four patterns, that opens up a whole new world of licks.

The extended box, shown here in fifth position, comprises notes on the top three strings, including two that are part of the root-position box pattern.

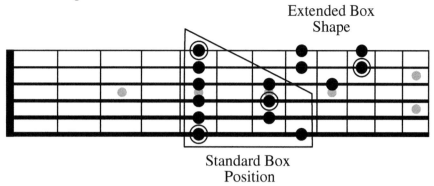

Strictly speaking, four of the five notes are also sounded in the root-position box. For example, using A as our root, the E note at the ninth fret of the third string is the same as the E note at the fifth fret on the second string. In fact, the only note in the extended box that's *not* in the root-position box is the highest note on the first string, in this case, the D at the tenth fret on the first string. As such, when you play the A minor pentatonic scale using the extended box, you need to make a position shift so that you don't repeat notes. Here's the scale as it lays out in tab, with recommended fingerings.

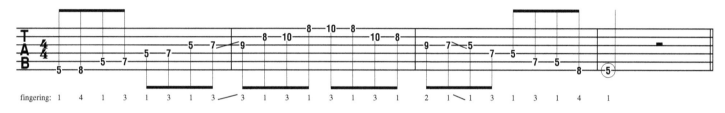

 Now, let's take a look at a couple of licks that take advantage of the extended box. The first one stays strictly in the box and uses a couple of quarter-step bends for a bluesy feel.

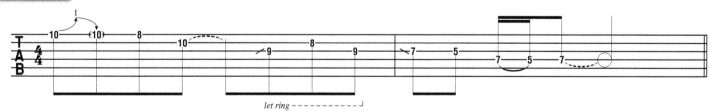

 This extended shape is often combined with the box position in the same lick, as in this one.

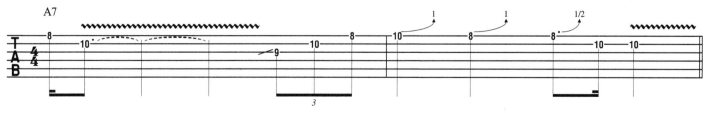

The extended box is often referred to as the "Albert King box," so named because players cop many of his signature licks in this three-fret area. (King himself played very unconventionally with an altered tuning and the guitar strung "upside down.") The next lick is a prime example.

The very first lick—the rapid move from the ♭3rd (C) to the root (A)—is vintage King, a move that has been used by countless blues guitarists since, to equally great effect. Note also the half-step bend in measure 2. The result of that bend is a C♯ note, which is the *major* 3rd and technically does not belong in the A minor pentatonic scale. That being said, the musical tension created by including the major 3rd in a minor scale lick is essentially the rock upon which the blues was built.

An absolute master of inserting the major 3rd into minor pentatonic scales, especially in the extended box, is the legendary king of the blues, B.B. King. This next example, which comprises the first three-and-a-half measures of his solo in the 1966 classic "Sweet Sixteen," demonstrates King's mastery of the extended box as well as his use of savory major 3rds.

"SWEET SIXTEEN"
B.B. King

Words and Music by B.B. King
and Joe Bihari

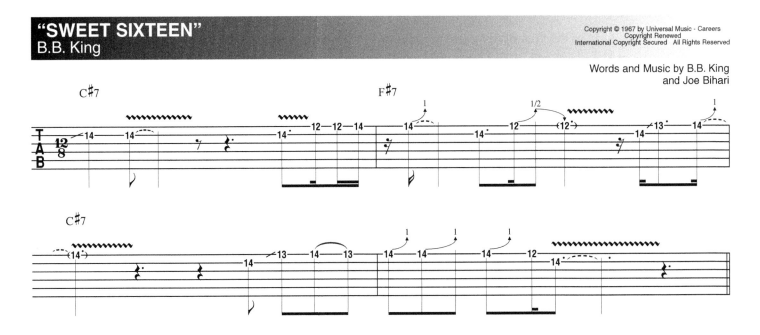

Finally, to close out this chapter, here are the first four bars from Stevie Ray Vaughan's cover of the Elmore James classic "The Sky Is Crying." This short but rich excerpt contains some of the most famous phrases ever constructed from the extended box, along with one of Vaughan's favorite licks from the root-position box as well.

"THE SKY IS CRYING"
Stevie Ray Vaughan

Words and Music by
Elmore James

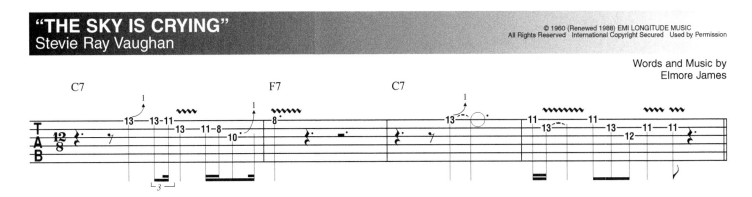

MODES

The modes of the major scale represent one of the most sought after banks of knowledge among budding lead guitarists. Through the years, the *modes*, as they've become simply known, have even taken on a sort of mystical aura, where guitarists who do not understand or use them hold a certain reverence for those who do. And while a solid grasp of the modes and how they work can certainly make you a better guitarist, their reputation is not really deserved. In fact, modes really aren't that difficult to understand, and with some practice, they can quickly become your best friend in your improvisations.

When people discuss "the modes," they're typically referring to the modes of the major scale. The major scale has seven modes, one for each of its seven notes. Here they are, in numerical order.

1. Ionian	**5. Mixolydian**
2. Dorian	**6. Aeolian**
3. Phrygian	**7. Locrian**
4. Lydian	

Take the time to memorize not only their names but also the numerical order in which they appear. Some people like to use a mnemonic like "**I** **D**on't **P**articularly **L**ike **M**odes **A** **L**ot," or "**I** **D**on't **P**lay **L**icks **M**ade **A**round **L**ocrian," to help them remember the first letter of each mode in proper order.

 Once you've got the names and numerical order memorized, we're going to show you a simple, four-step process that will enable you to instantly find any mode. To demonstrate the process, let's say we're improvising over a Dm7 chord, and wish to use the D Phrygian mode.

STEP 1: Determine the mode number
Phrygian is our goal mode, and Phrygian is the third mode of the major scale, so it's number is "3."

STEP 2: Assign that mode number to a root
We're playing over a Dm7 chord, so our root is D. So we assign the mode number, 3, to the root D, which means D=3.

STEP 3: Count down the major scale formula from the assigned mode number to 1
In this case, we've determined that D is the 3rd degree of the major scale in question. So if we count backward from the 3rd (D), using the major scale formula (see page 4), we first descend a whole step, to the 2nd (C), and then another whole step, to 1, or the root (B♭).

STEP 4: Play major scale of 1, but start on chord root letter
In our example, you'll now play the notes of the B♭ major scale, but start and end on D, instead of B♭. In doing so, you're playing the D Phrygian mode.

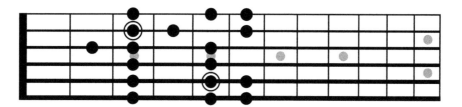

Now let's play each mode, and more importantly, learn when to use them, as we practice the four-step location process in different keys. For this lesson, we'll use C as the root for each mode. We'll begin, of course, with mode #1, the Ionian mode.

The Ionian Mode

You may not realize it, but you've already learned the Ionian mode—it's simply the major scale. What makes it the Ionian *mode*, however, is the context in which you play it. When you play a major scale over a major chord of the same root, or over a chord progression in that root's key, you're playing the Ionian mode.

Because Ionian is the first mode, you can skip Step 3, and just begin playing the C major scale from the root, C.

By now, you should be familiar with the sound of the major scale, and thus, the Ionian mode, from the licks found in the Major Scale lesson of this book. But here are two more Ionian-based phrases, for good measure. The first is in the style of Journey guitarist Neal Schon, king of the major-scale melodic rock solo.

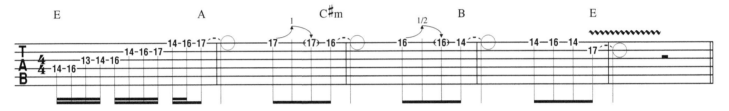

Next, we take a page from another of the major-key melodic greats: Pink Floyd's David Gilmour. This Ionian-based phrase is reminiscent of his work in "Comfortably Numb."

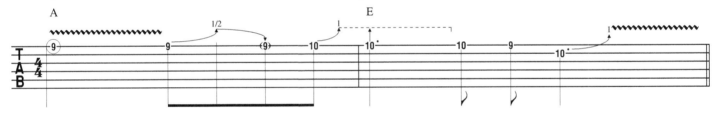

The Dorian Mode

Typically associated with improvisation in jazz settings over ii–V–I progressions, the Dorian mode is equally effective in rock settings. A colorful alternative to the natural minor scale, the Dorian mode's natural 6th degree provides a bluesy classic-rock sound over minor chords and progressions.

To find C Dorian, follow the steps. Dorian is mode 2, so you assign numeral 2 to the note C. Then, you count backward from 2 to 1, or one whole step; this takes you from C to B♭. Finally, you play the B♭ major scale, starting and ending on C, to play C Dorian.

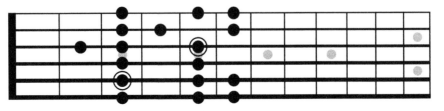

You can also think of the Dorian mode as a major scale with flatted 3rd and 7th degrees: 1–2–♭3–4–5–6–♭7.

One of the finest practitioners of the Dorian mode in classic rock is Carlos Santana. Here is a Santana-style E Dorian lick over a i–IV (Em7–A) progression typical of his songs.

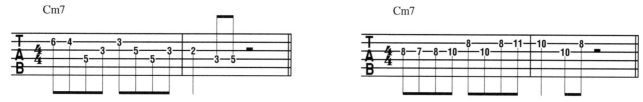

As we mentioned, the Dorian mode is most often heard in jazz improvisation, over minor seventh chords. Here are two stock C Dorian licks over a Cm7 chord.

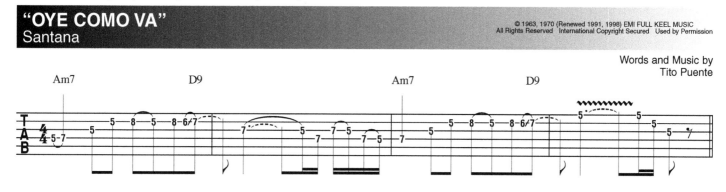

The essence of the Dorian mode is a minor i chord and a major IV chord. In "Oye Como Va," Carlos Santana outlines these pithy changes in the beginning of his famous solo.

"OYE COMO VA"
Santana

Words and Music by
Tito Puente

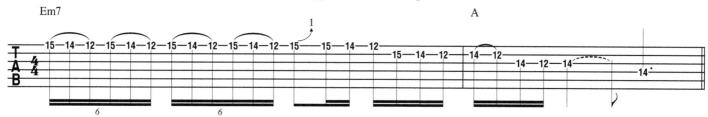

Phrygian Mode

With a darker sound than its Dorian and Aeolian cousins, the Phrygian mode is a favorite of heavy metal guitarists, for its half-step interval from the root to the $\flat$2nd.

Phrygian is the third mode, so using the four-step process, we determine that C Phrygian is the same as $A\flat$ major, only starting on the C note.

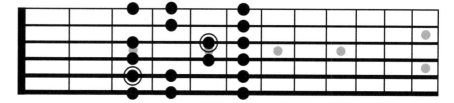

Another way to look at the Phrygian mode is as a major scale with lowered 2nd, 3rd, 6th, and 7th degrees: 1–$\flat$2–$\flat$3–4–5–$\flat$6–$\flat$7.

Because the Phrygian mode is a minor scale, it's played over minor chords. In rock settings, you'll want to use the Phrygian mode over i–$\flat$II progressions. Here's a high-octane legato lick using the E Phrygian mode over an E5–F5 progression.

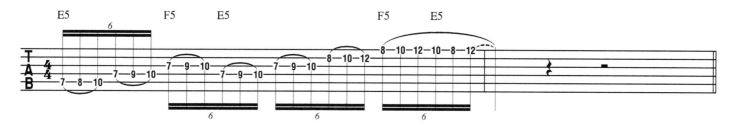

The Lydian Mode

The fourth mode of the major scale, Lydian is a major mode with a less-traditional sound than Ionian. The only difference between Lydian and the major scale, or Ionian mode, is that Lydian has a raised 4th degree. This small but significant difference lends the mode a "dreamy" and anticipatory character.

Using the four-step process to find C Lydian, we find that it's the same as the G major scale, starting on C.

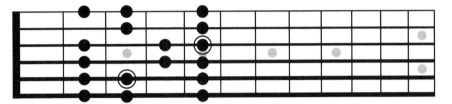

As we mentioned just a few sentences ago, the Lydian mode is the same as the major scale, only with a raised 4th: 1–2–3–#4–5–6–7.

Used over a static major-chord vamp or a classic I–II Lydian progression, the Lydian mode offers a refreshing change of pace from the consonance of the Ionian mode.

And in the hands of masters like Joe Satriani and Steve Vai, the Lydian mode can move mountains. Here are the first four bars of the intro to Vai's "The Riddle."

"THE RIDDLE"
Steve Vai

By Steve Vai

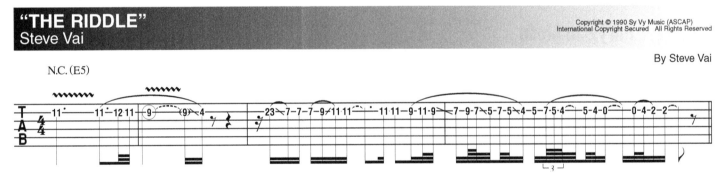

The Mixolydian Mode

The fifth mode of the major scale, the Mixolydian mode is the perfect fit for soloing over dominant 7th chords. And because dominant 7ths are frequently found in styles ranging from rock to jazz to blues to classical, the Mixolydian mode can be your best friend.

Using C as our root and following the four-step process, you'll find that C Mixolydian is the same as F major, starting on C.

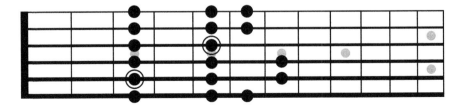

You can also think of the Mixolydian mode as a major scale with a ♭7th degree, which, depending on the context in which it's used, gives it either a bluesy sound, or the vibe of a slightly darkened major scale. The latter is demonstrated below, in an E Mixolydian modern-rock riff. The use of the droning low E string really helps drive home the Mixolydian sound.

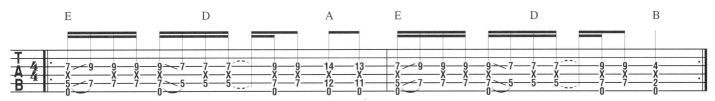

The Fab Four crafted one of the most famous Mixolydian riffs in rock for "Day Tripper." Note the passing G♮ for an added bluesy touch.

"DAY TRIPPER"
The Beatles

Words and Music by John Lennon
and Paul McCartney

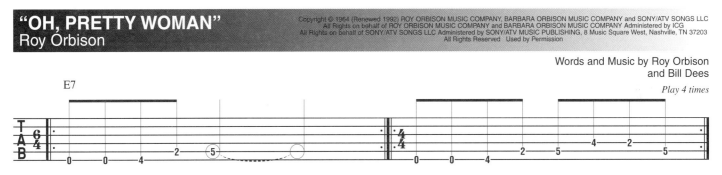

And perhaps *the* most famous Mixolydian riff in pop music history is Roy Orbison's timeless hit, "Oh, Pretty Woman."

"OH, PRETTY WOMAN"
Roy Orbison

Words and Music by Roy Orbison
and Bill Dees

Play 4 times

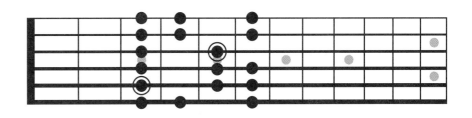

Aeolian Mode

Like the Ionian mode, the Aeolian mode is another with which you're already familiar, only you know it by its more common name: the natural minor scale. Recall that way back on page 11, you learned how to find the *relative minor* scale; you use the same process to find the Aeolian mode. Or, you can use the four-step process as follows.

Using C as our root, we know that Aeolian is the sixth mode of the major scale, so we assign the numeral "6" to the note C. Then you count backward from 6 to 1, using the major scale formula, which brings you to E♭. So if you play the notes of the E♭ major scale, beginning on C, you've got the C Aeolian mode.

Alternatively, as you learned with the relative minor scale, you can think of the Aeolian mode as a major scale with flatted 3rd, 6th, and 7th degrees: 1–2–♭3–4–5–♭6–♭7.

We already played a ton of licks and riffs using the Aeolian mode, or natural minor scale, back in the Minor Scale lesson of this book. So to further examine the Aeolian mode here, we're going to present it in a light not often discussed—how it fits into jazz improvisation. Most jazzers tend to stay away from the Aeolian mode, thinking it too pedestrian-sounding. But as these licks demonstrate, that's not always the case.

This first lick comprises a series of Fm, Cm, and Gm7 arpeggios from the C Aeolian mode, played over a static Cm7 chord. Even though all of the notes are found in the C Aeolian mode, grouping them together into these arpeggios is a common improvisation tool in jazz.

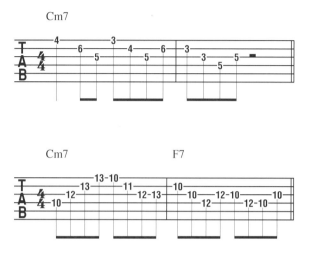

Our second jazz lick puts the C Aeolian mode to work over the Cm7 chord in a Cm7–F7 progression, which is a ii–V in the key of B♭ major. Though the Dorian mode is generally the scale of choice over ii–V progressions, the ♭6th of the Aeolian mode, in this case an A♭, helps to create a jazzy chromatic sequence leading to the natural A note that starts measure 2, drawn from the F Mixolydian mode.

The Locrian Mode

The seventh mode of the major scale is the Locrian mode. Quite honestly, it's very rarely used in rock, pop, blues, or country music. About the only time it ever rears its ugly head is in a minor-key jazz progression, when a m7♭5 chord serves as a ii chord. And when that happens, you'll almost always find the i chord next to it. Which means you'll get the Locrian sound you need for the m7♭5 simply by playing the i chord's Aeolian mode. For example, if you see a B♭m7–Cm7♭5 change, just play B♭ Aeolian over both chords!

That being said, in the interest of being thorough, here's the four-step process for finding the C Locrian mode. As the seventh mode, we count backward from 7 to 1, using the major scale formula, to arrive at D♭ major. So if you play the D♭ major scale, from C to C, you're playing C Locrian.

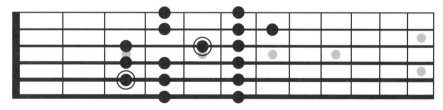

You can also think of the Locrian mode as a major scale with flatted 2nd, 3rd, 5th, 6th, and 7th degrees.

And as an even easier alternative for finding the Locrian mode, simply play the major scale that's one half step above the Locrian mode's root. For example, to play C Locrian, simply play a D♭ major scale, starting on C. Here is a jazzy example using the C Locrian mode over a Cm7♭5 chord in a ii–V–i progression in B♭ minor.

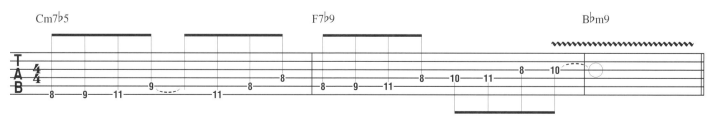

More Modal Fingerings

In the previous pages, we presented all of the modes with the root, C, sitting on the fifth string at the third fret, so you could easily visualize the differences between each one. Although each of those scale shapes is usable and movable, they're not all necessarily the most commonly used fingerings. So here are more popular and useful fingerings for each of the seven modes of the major scale.

Patterns for Ionian

Patterns for Dorian

Patterns for Phrygian

Patterns for Lydian

Patterns for Mixolydian

Patterns for Aeolian

Patterns for Locrian

To close out *Guitar Scales and Modes*, here are two scale exercises that essentially cover every scale type presented in this book. The first is a modal exercise that takes you through all seven modes of F major, which means you're also playing the major (Ionian) and minor (Aeolian) scales covered in the first two chapters of the book. Using a metronome to keep time, practice this once a day, moving it up one fret each new day, and use alternate picking to navigate the exercise.

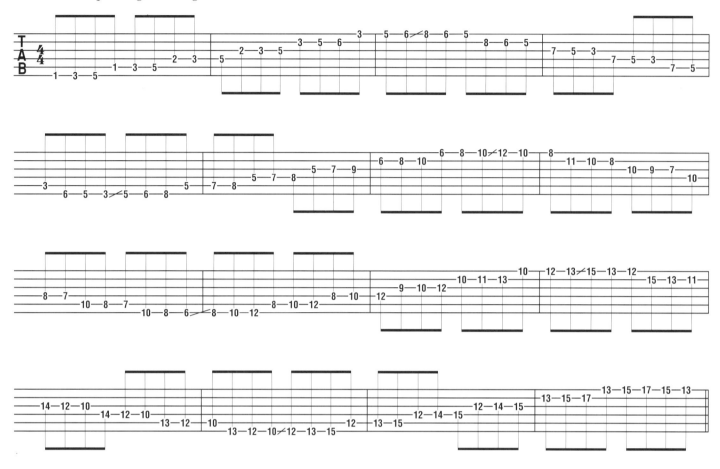

The second and final exercise takes you through all five fingering patterns of the minor pentatonic scale, in the key of F, starting with the root-position box pattern you learned in the Minor Pentatonic Scale lesson. In addition to playing through this exercise in its entirety, break it down and practice each of the five patterns (separated by diagonal "slide" slashes in the tab) on its own. Again, use alternate picking and a metronome.

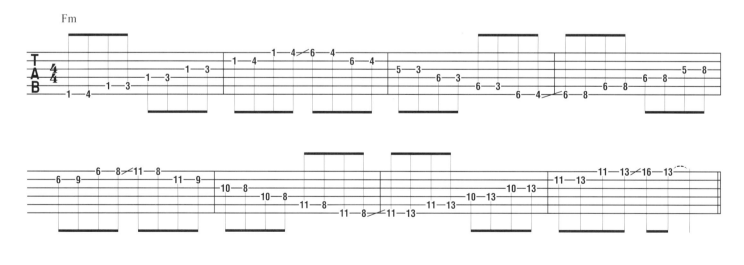